COUNTRY

Formal Name: Taiwan (台灣); formally, Republic of China (Chung-hua Min-kuo—中華民國).

Short Form: Taiwan (台灣).

Term for Citizen(s): Chinese (Hua-jen—華人); Taiwanese (T'ai-wan-jen—台灣人).

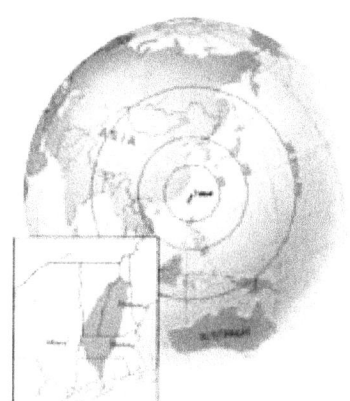

Click to Enlarge Image

Capital: The capital of central administration of Taiwan is Taipei (T'ai-pei—台北—literally, Taiwan North), located in T'ai-pei County in the north. Since 1967, Taipei has been administratively separate from Taiwan Province.

Major Cities: The largest city is Taipei, with 2.6 million inhabitants in 2004. Other large cities are Kao-hsiung, with 1.5 million, and T'ai-chung, with 1 million. Fifteen other cities have populations ranging from 216,000 to 749,000 inhabitants.

National Public Holidays: Founding Day (January 1, marking the founding of the Republic of China in 1912); Lunar New Year (also called Spring Festival, based on the lunar calendar, occurs between January 21 and February 19 and is preceded by eight days of preparatory festivities); Peace Memorial Day (February 28, commemorating the February 28, 1947, incident); Tomb Sweeping Day (Ching Ming, April 4); Dragon Boat Festival (fifth day of the fifth lunar month, movable date in June); Mid-Autumn Festival (15th day of the eighth lunar month, movable date in September); and Double Tenth National Day (October 10, also called Republic Day, commemorates the anniversary of the Chinese revolution in 1911 and the date from which years are sometimes counted). Also marked but not as national holidays and closure of government offices are Youth Day (March 29), Women's and Children's Day (April 4), Labor Day (May 1), Mother's Day (May 8), Father's Day (August 8), Ghost Festival (15th day of the seventh lunar month, movable date in August or September), Armed Forces Day (September 3), Teachers' Day and Confucius's Birthday (September 28), Taiwan Retrocession Day (October 25, marks return by Japan of Taiwan to Chinese rule in 1945), Sun Yat-sen's Birthday (November 12), and Constitution Day (December 25).

Flag:
The Republic of China flag has a crimson field with a dark blue rectangle representing the sky in the upper hoist-side corner and bearing a white sun with 12 triangular rays. The blue, white, and crimson represent the Three Principles of the People (San Min Chu I —nationalism, democracy,

Click to Enlarge Image

and social well-being). The 12 points of the white sun represent the 12 two-hour periods of the day, symbolizing unceasing progress. The white sun and blue sky symbol has been used since 1895. The flag has been in use since 1921 and was adopted by the new national government in 1928.

HISTORICAL BACKGROUND

Prehistory: Taiwan has had human settlement for at least 15,000 years, dating to the Paleolithic age, and evidence of Neolithic agrarian settlements, similar to those of coastal China, dating from 4000 to 2500 B.C., have also been found. Because there was no land bridge to mainland Asia, the supposition is that these Neolithic peoples were seafarers as well as agriculturalists. There are several theories as to the origins of the aboriginal, Austronesian-speaking peoples living in Taiwan today. Some scholars believe that the first people to populate Taiwan were Malayo-Polynesians, specifically from Indonesia—peoples of a southern origin. Others argue for a northern origin—tribal peoples from southeastern mainland China—in support of the argument that Taiwan has always been a part of China. Some have posited Taiwan as the origin of the Austronesian languages, a position supporting an early Neolithic migration from southeastern China followed by independent development in Taiwan.

Mainland and European Arrivals: Mainland Chinese began to trade with the aborigines around the fourteenth century. Substantial numbers of Chinese migrants did not arrive until after the arrival in Taiwan in 1624 of the Portuguese, who called it Ilha Formosa (Beautiful Island). Spain established fortified harbor outposts in northern Taiwan in 1626 and 1628, followed by the construction of connecting roads and missionary activities. The Dutch arrived in 1632 and established themselves at several outposts, with trade with the mainland as their main goal. By 1642 the Dutch had easily supplanted the Spanish presence, but then both the Portuguese and Dutch were expelled by a Chinese pirate and trader, Cheng Ch'eng-kung (Zheng Chenggong; also known as Koxinga), in 1662. Under Cheng's administration, emigration, mostly from Fujian (Fu-chien) and Guangdong (Kwang-tung), was encouraged, and by 1664 the Chinese population had reached about 50,000; within 20 years, it had doubled. Mainlander settlement forced the aborigines from their traditional lands in the western plains up into the central mountains. There they fought to keep Chinese settlers out, and occasionally they raided lowland settlements.

Qing Period: Cheng Ch'eng-kung and his descendants, who were loyal to the former Ming Dynasty (1368–1643), controlled Taiwan for 20 years. In 1683 military forces of the new Qing Dynasty (1644–1911) took control of the P'eng-hu (Pescadores) Islands and wrested Taiwan from the Cheng family. Two years later, they made it a prefecture of Fujian Province. Although the Qing banned migration to Taiwan, many mainlanders were still attracted to its fertile soil. The economy was based on trade, and expansion shifted from the southwestern coast and plains around T'ai-nan (which had become a treaty port) to the north around Taipei, the new provincial capital. As Taiwan opened to foreign trade, European and American treaty port officials, merchants, and missionaries arrived in significant numbers. Economic and social transformation was accompanied by population growth and urbanization and, in 1885, Taiwan was raised to provincial status.

Japanese Colonial Period: Under the Treaty of Shimonoseki (April 17, 1895) following China's defeat by Japan in the First Sino-Japanese War (1894–95), Taiwan and the P'eng-hu Islands were ceded to Japan. Tokyo saw Taiwan as a source of raw materials for Japan's industries, a colonial market for Japanese goods, and a model for economic growth. Taiwan also provided Japan with an important strategic outpost and southern defensive position. However, in May 1895, a short-lived Taiwan Republic was proclaimed by the Chinese governor with the hope of Western intervention. After the governor quietly departed, remnant Qing troops, militia forces, and armed partisan bands engaged in a five-month-long resistance that brought further wartime damage. Over the next seven years, Japanese forces continued to pacify the island.

Japanese administrators conducted land surveys and brought order to the landholding system. The tax base began to improve as urban enterprises developed and a new class of owner-cultivators developed in rural areas. By the early twentieth century, railroads linked the northern and southern parts of the island, and new roads served interior areas. The Japanese-owned sugarcane industry became important. The population grew during the Japanese period from 3 million in 1905 to 9 million in 1945. Some of this growth came from the continued influx of laborers brought from the mainland. In 1920 the first Taiwanese-inspired political movement was formed, ultimately advocating a form of autonomy for the island. The reaction from Japan was negative, but the movement, led briefly by the New People's Society and then the League for the Establishment of a Taiwan Parliament, continued until 1934, when it was suppressed by Japan's emerging ultranationalist forces. Even though an increasingly skilled and better-educated population had emerged, Taiwan's population was kept from political participation throughout the colonial period. Rule at times was harsh and repressive, especially after the end of the rule of civilian governors-general (1915–36). When Japan went on a war footing against China (1936–45), Taiwan became a staging area for the invasion of southern China. The wartime economy brought construction, growth of heavy industry, use of modern technology, and development of a skilled industrial labor force. Taiwanese troops and medical personnel were sent to various parts of the wartime theater. The sudden end of the war was troubling to many Taiwanese. Some had been loyal to Japan; others, full of hatred of colonial rule, looked forward to the return of Chinese rule. Taiwan self-determination was not offered as a consideration. Nevertheless, modern Taiwanese scholars see this period as an intrinsic part of their historical legacy, a period that brought the island into the modern age and began to define a separate identity from mainland China.

Postwar Occupation: The military forces of the Republic of China under the Kuomintang (Chinese Nationalist Party—Chung-kuo Kuo-min-tang—usually shorted to Kuomintang, KMT) arrived in Taiwan after the war and started to erase all vestiges of Japanese rule and to bring the island under Nationalist Chinese political, economic, and cultural influence. Rather than treating Taiwan as a liberated area, the KMT forces confronted the local population as enemy collaborators. Businesses were looted and goods were seized as KMT military officers and politicians took charge. The abolition of the use of widely spoken Japanese and the imposition of Mandarin Chinese led to communications and political problems. Taiwanese political groups and the media sought influence, but mainlanders predominated in the key provincial administrative positions. Provincial and local assembly elections took place in 1946, but the Taiwanese found their elected bodies had only limited powers. Decolonization and reintegration were proving difficult, and the KMT regime was turning out to be just as exploitative and controlling as the

Japanese had been but less competent. Resentment was on the rise. When unarmed demonstrators protested the corrupt KMT occupation and overthrew the provincial administration in early 1947, they were violently suppressed in what has become known as the February 28 Incident. A military reign of terror ensued, and an estimated 8,000 to 10,000 (some say 100,000) people were killed and some 30,000 wounded. To commemorate this bloody event, February 28 has, since 1995, been marked as a national memorial day.

Taiwan under KMT Rule: Following the KMT defeat by the Chinese Communist Party (CCP) on the mainland in 1949 and faced with instability on the island on which he had to reestablish his base, KMT leader Chiang Kai-shek (Jiang Jieshi, 1888–1975) and his party reformed their regime politically and established a "socialist-minded state control" over heavy industry. Mainland refugees took over most aspects of governance, the economy, and the education system. The "loss of China" in 1949 and the onset of the Korean War (1950–53) against communist-run North Korea and its Chinese ally impelled the United States to help the Republic of China on Taiwan to become a bulwark against communism. The U.S. 7th Fleet was assigned to patrol the Taiwan Strait to prevent an invasion of Taiwan. The United States provided economic and military aid, and in 1954 a mutual security treaty was signed with the Republic of China as part of Washington's Cold War policy of containment of the Beijing regime. But military aid was limited to what Taiwan needed to defend itself against the People's Republic of China and not to support Chiang Kai-shek's dream of "returning to the mainland."

The government established on Taiwan in 1949 had national and provincial levels. The national level, with elected and appointed officials brought from the mainland, represented itself as the Republic of China in international forums and ostensibly prepared for a return to rule over all of the mainland. At the onset, the KMT controlled Taiwan, small offshore islands belonging to Fujian and Zhejiang provinces on the mainland, and Hainan Island, south of Guangdong Province. Although they lost control of Hainan and Zhejiang's Chou-shan Islands in 1950 and Zhejiang's Ta-chen Island in 1955, the islands appertaining to Fujian—Kinmen (Chin-men, Jinmen, or Quemoy) and Matsu (Ma-tzu)—were still under the control of the Republic of China in 2005. Beginning in the early 1950s, county, municipal, and provincial—but not national— elections were held. In 1959 the Taiwan Provincial Assembly was established, a situation that gave the Taiwan people an opportunity to participate in provincial life even though the central government maintained three parliamentary bodies—the National Assembly, the Legislative Yuan, and the Control Yuan, with seats largely held by mainlanders who had been elected prior to 1949—whose interests were not local but concerned a national territory that they no longer controlled. The tenures of these holdover representatives were extended by presidential order, but as they died off, the regime was forced to hold an election in 1969 to fill the empty seats. The two-term limitation on the presidency was amended by the National Assembly in 1960 to allow Chiang Kai-shek to remain in office during "the period of communist rebellion." Local politics were controlled by the KMT through influence exerted on local politicians and manipulation of elections.

In the 1950s, the government transferred industries seized from the Japanese in 1945 to private management. Land reform also took place and greatly reduced tenancy. By the 1960s, following a decade of manufacture of consumer goods for domestic consumption, Taiwan shifted to the export trade, using low-paid labor to produce consumer electronics and other desirable goods.

Americans and Japanese invested heavily in Taiwan's industries, and export processing zones were established in Kao-hsiung and T'ai-chung, replete with tax incentives and export-tax exemptions. The Second Indochina War (1954–75) also stimulated the island's economy. As further shifts to heavy industries, such as steel and petrochemicals, took place, the island became increasingly urbanized. Exports grew eightfold during the 1960s, as Taiwan became the world's fastest growing economy. Personal income also increased, and the government began investing more in education. In 1965 the population stood at 12.6 million, and by 1985 had reached 19.2 million. By 1988 Taiwan's gross national product (GNP) had reached US$95 billion, and per capita GNP, at US$4,800, was 10 times that of mainland China.

Despite these substantial economic advances—which brought Taiwan the characterization as one of the "Four Tigers" (along with South Korea, Hong Kong, and Singapore) of economic prowess in Asia—the Republic of China did not fare well in the international political milieu. Although a permanent member of the United Nations (UN) Security Council when the UN was formed in 1945, the Republic of China was ousted from the China seat in 1971 by a vote of the UN General Assembly. At the same time, the United States was changing its own policy of containing the People's Republic of China, which led to further isolation of Taiwan. Washington's recognition of Taipei ended in 1979, but quasi-official relations continued under other arrangements.

On the domestic front, the prosperity Taiwan enjoyed brought increasing pressure for political reform. As the original generation of mainlanders retired from positions of authority in the party, government, and military, they increasingly were replaced by Taiwan-born individuals. Even though a few independent Taiwanese politicians were elected to local and provincial positions, the KMT continued to hold a monopoly of central power. When Chiang Kei-shek died in 1975, he was succeeded by his son, Premier Chiang Ching-kuo (Jiang Jingguo), as head of the party and president of the Republic of China.

The younger, more liberal Chiang began "Taiwanizing" the KMT and the government, bringing in those who shared his views on socioeconomic modernization. The political door was cracked open, and soon independents (non-party—*tang-wai* or *dangwai*) were winning numerous seats in the Taiwan Provincial Assembly and in local elections. Things did not always go well, however. On December 10, 1979, there was a violent clash between *tang-wai* demonstrators and KMT-hired troublemakers and local police in Kao-hsiung. During the next eight years, government attempts to repress political activism were met with renewed middle-class activism, which eventually led to reform within the KMT. Emboldened, the *tang-wai* activists defied the government's ban on establishing new political parties and founded the Democratic Progressive Party (Minzhu Jinpu Dang, abbreviated as Minjindang; DPP) in September 1986. Chiang resisted his conservative colleagues in the KMT and allowed the DPP to stand. In October 1986, Chiang facilitated a resolution to end martial law, which had been in effect since 1948. In December 1986, the first legal two-party Legislative Yuan election was held, and the DPP won 12 of the 73 open seats. Chiang also made liberalizing gestures to Beijing by allowing Republic of China citizens to visit the mainland.

When he died in January 1988, Chiang Ching-kuo was succeeded by his vice president, Lee Teng-hui, a Taiwanese-born and Japanese- and American-educated academician who had previously served as the appointed governor of Taiwan Province. Although the KMT won the most seats in the 1989 elections, the DPP made major advances. The KMT, however, was becoming increasingly factionalized over political reform and foreign policy. Lee was elected president by the National Assembly in his own right in 1990, but a conservative career military man—"one-China" policy supporter and law-and-order advocate Hau Pei-tsun—was elected premier. This situation further factionalized the KMT and emboldened the DPP to issue statements promoting Taiwan independence. Lee Tung-hui continued his reforms by transforming the National Assembly to a smaller (327 seats instead of 613), popularly elected legislature with four-year instead of six-year terms. Another parliamentary body, the Legislative Yuan, was reduced from 220 seats to 161. The DPP's platform called for a plebiscite on independence, but voters, uneasy with this concept, overwhelmingly supported KMT candidates in the December 1990 National Assembly elections (254 seats for the KMT to 66 for the DPP).

KMT factional politics eventually meant losses for the conservatives led by Hau Pei-tsun and victory for Lee Tung-hui. In 1991 Lee declared an end to the hostilities with the mainland regime, abandoned the long-standing claims that the Taiwan authorities governed mainland China, and stated that Taiwan no longer disputed the fact that the People's Republic of China controlled mainland China. KMT power was slipping, as it won only 102 seats to 50 seats for the DPP and 9 other seats for *tang-wai* candidates in the 1992 Legislative Yuan elections. The DPP then joined with the New KMT Alliance, a coalition of anti-Lee, reform-minded, pro-reunification KMT legislators, to pass the Sunshine Bill, an act to force legislators and bureaucrats to disclose their financial assets. In July 1993, the New KMT Alliance broke with the KMT to form the New Party (Hsin Tang or Xindang, initially the Chinese New Party or Zhongguo Xindang). An amendment to the constitution in 1994 led in March 1996 to the election of Lee Tung-hui as Taiwan's first popularly elected president, with Premier Lien Chan as vice president and the KMT winning 54 percent of the vote. In the National Assembly elections held at the same time, the KMT won only a slim majority, 183 seats to the DPP's 99 seats and the New Party's 56 seats. During his second term, Lee said that a "special state-to-state relationship" existed in Taiwan's relations with China. In doing so, he incurred the wrath of Beijing, and new cross-strait tensions set in.

A New Political Era: The presidential election of March 2000 was a momentous one for Taiwan. DPP candidate Chen Shui-bian, who had served as the elected mayor of Taipei from 1994 to 1998, defeated KMT candidate Lien Chan and the more-than 50-year era of KMT dominance was over. Although the DPP won the larger share of seats in the Legislative Yuan, the KMT's alliance with the People First Party (Qinmindang, a KMT breakaway party) gave the KMT de facto control. Thus, the new era also meant one of divided government and impediments for the new DPP administration. Further complications arose to thwart the DPP's efforts soon after Chen's inauguration in May 2000, when the international high-technology industry began experiencing severe problems and orders from Taiwan quickly and substantially decreased. In 2003, as the economy began to recover, the severe acute respiratory syndrome (SARS) crisis hit Taiwan, temporarily shaking confidence. Despite the inauguration of Lunar New Year tourist flights from Taiwan to China via Hong Kong and Macau, Beijing continued to be wary of the DPP and refused to engage in suggested government-to-government talks or anything else relating to direct links that might improve Chen Shui-bian's chances at winning a second term in 2004. Chen ran a successful campaign, and, despite an assassination attempt on March 19, 2004, he went on to win a second term in the March 20, 2004, election. In the

December 2004 Legislative Yuan elections, the DPP won more seats than any other party and was allied with another major party, the Taiwan Solidarity Union (Taiwan Tuanjie Lianmeng; TSU) in the Pan-Green alliance. However, the KMT-People First Party coalition (known as the Pan-Blue alliance) had greater strength in overall numbers and thus continued to control the legislature.

GEOGRAPHY

Location: Taiwan is located in East Asia and situated on two strategic straits, the Taiwan Strait, facing the southeastern coast of China, and the Luzon Strait, which connects the Pacific Ocean with the South China Sea north of the Philippines. Besides the island of Taiwan and six small islands that appertain to it off the Pacific Ocean (east) coast, the government also controls the P'eng-hu Islands (64 islands southwest of Taiwan in the middle of the Taiwan Strait, also known as the Pescadores). On the west side of the Taiwan Strait, Taiwan controls Kinmen (12 islands, also rendered as Chin-men, Jinmen, and Quemoy), 182 nautical miles west of Taiwan; and Matsu (10 islands, also rendered Ma-tzu), 114 nautical miles west of Taiwan. Both Kinmen and Matsu appertain to China's Fu-chien (Fujian) Province. Taiwan also has effective jurisdiction over the Tung-sha (Dongsha or Pratas) Islands and Taiping Island (Ita Abu Island) in the Nan-sha (Spratly Islands) in the South China Sea.

Click to Enlarge Image

Size: Taiwan's total area is 35,980 square kilometers, of which 32,260 square kilometers are land and 3,720 square kilometers are water.

Land Boundaries: Taiwan and other islands under its jurisdiction have no land boundaries.

Length of Coastline: The total coastline of Taiwan measures 1,566 kilometers. The East China Sea is to the north, the Pacific Ocean is to the east, the Philippine Sea is to the southeast, the South China Sea is to the southwest, and the Taiwan Strait is to the west.

Maritime Claims: Taipei claims a territorial sea of 12 nautical miles and an exclusive economic zone of 200 nautical miles. Taiwan is involved in a complex dispute with China, Malaysia, Philippines, Vietnam, and possibly Brunei over islands in the South China Sea. These include the Nan-sha (Spratly) Islands, Hsi-sha (Sisha or Xisha, Paracel) Islands, Tung-sha (Dongsha, Pratas) Islands, and Chung-sha (Zhongsha, or Macclesfield Bank) Islands. Taiwan and China also lay claim to a small archipelago 75 nautical miles northeast of Taiwan, called Tiao-yü T'ai (or Diaoyutai; known to Japan as the Senkaku Islands), which are under Japanese administration.

Topography: The eastern two-thirds of Taiwan, facing the East China Sea and Pacific Ocean, is mostly rugged mountains, which run north to south and cover about 63 percent of the island. The T'ai-tung Mountains in the east have an average elevation of 1,000 meters. The Chung-yang Shan (Central Mountains) range dominates the island, with some 200 peaks that exceed 3,000 meters. The highest point at 3,952 meters above sea level is Yü-shan (Jade Mountain, also known as Mount Morrison) in the Yü-shan Shan Mountains (Jade Mountains), on the southwest side of the Chung-yang Shan Mountains. Volcanic peaks are found in the Ta-t'un Shan Mountain area near Chi-lung (Keelung) and Taipei. To the west of the Chung-yang Shan are rolling hills that descend to gently rolling alluvial plains and the Taiwan Strait. This relatively flat region extends some 300 kilometers north to south but is no wider than 50 kilometers at its broadest reach. The lowest point is zero meters above sea level along parts of the coast.

Principal Rivers: Taiwan has some 151 rivers and streams with short, steep descents on the east side of the island and longer but still steep descents into the western alluvial plains. The Cho-shui River is the longest at 187 kilometers, with a drainage basin of 3,157 square kilometers. The 171-kilometer-long Kao-p'ing River has the largest drainage basin (3,257 square kilometers). The Taipei Basin is drained by the 159-kilometer-long Tan-shui River, which once was deep enough for ocean-going sailing ships but now is restricted to shallow-draft boats.

Climate: The climate is tropical and marine. There is a rainy season during the southwest monsoon, from June to August. Cloudiness is persistent and extensive year-round. Typhoons regularly hit Taiwan during July to September each year. The lowest monthly average rainfall is normally in November, at 66 millimeters; the greatest is in August, with 305 millimeters. Most rain falls between May and October, and the driest months are between November and February. The mean annual rainfall in the Taiwan area is 2,483 millimeters, with heavier rainfalls in the north and south and slightly lower levels in the east and central regions. Average temperatures range between 12° C and 18° C in the coldest month (February) and 24° C to 33° C in the hottest month (July).

Natural Resources: The most important natural resources are small deposits of asbestos, coal, limestone, marble, and natural gas.

Land Use: Twenty-four percent of the land is arable but has been diminishing since the late 1970s as a result of urbanization and industrialization. About 1 percent of the land is planted to permanent crops. The rest is categorized as "other."

Environmental Factors: Because of its location at the junction of the Manila Trench and the Ryukyu Trench along the west side of the Philippine Sea plate, Taiwan is susceptible to earthquakes. Large earthquakes occurred in Taiwan in 1935, 1986, and twice in 1999. Seasonal typhoons sometimes cause violent weather conditions leading to death and destruction. Five decades of rapid industrialization have caused considerable environmental damage to Taiwan. The resulting major concerns are air pollution, water pollution from industrial emissions, raw sewage, contamination of drinking water supplies, trade in endangered species, and low-level radioactive waste disposal. Taiwan's rivers are heavily polluted near the coast. The government's Environmental Protection Agency monitors environmental problems and requires environmental impact assessments from industrial and other potential polluters.

Time Zone: Taiwan is in one time zone (Asia/Taipei), 8 hours ahead of Greenwich Mean Time.

SOCIETY

Population: Taiwan's population was estimated in July 2004 at 22,749,838. The population at the most recent census (2000) stood at 22,300,929. The annual population growth rate is 0.64 percent. Estimates put Taiwan's population density at 705.2 persons per square kilometer in 2004, the second highest in the world after Bangladesh. The most densely populated area is Kaohsiung, with 9,827 persons per square kilometer; Taipei is second, with 9,720 persons per square kilometer. About 69 percent of the population lives in urban areas and 31 percent in rural areas.

Demography: According to estimates of Taiwan's age structure, 19.9 percent of the population is 0–14 years of age; 70.7 percent, 15–64 years of age; and 9.4 percent, 65 and older. Estimates made in 2004 indicate a birthrate of nearly 12.7 births per 1,000 population and a death rate of almost 6.3 deaths per 1,000. In 2004 life expectancy at birth was estimated at nearly 80.1 years for women and 74.3 for men, or 77.0 years total. The infant mortality rate was estimated at 6.5 per 1,000 live births, and the total fertility rate for 2004 was estimated at about 1.6 children per woman. The gender ratio at birth was 1.1 males to 1 female.

Migration: In the 1960s, numerous Taiwan residents left for educational and employment opportunities abroad in industrialized nations, but as Taiwan became an economic powerhouse in the 1980s and 1990s, many returned or stayed. Migration from Taiwan since the 1990s has been primarily to mainland China, mostly to Shanghai and Guangdong Province.

Ethnic Groups: Native-born Taiwanese, including Hakka (originally from upland areas of Guangdong and Fujian), make up 84 percent of the population. Mainland Chinese constitute 14 percent of the population and tribal aborigines about 2 percent. Since 1994, the aborigines, once referred to by the government as "mountain compatriots," "mountain people," or "Taiwanese aborigines," officially have been called *Yuan-chu-min* or "Taiwan aboriginal peoples." The Ministry of Interior reports that Taiwan has 12 major indigenous peoples: the Amis, Atayal, Bunun, Kavalan, Paiwan, Pinuyumayan or Punuyumayan, Rukai, Saisiyat, Thao, Truku, Tsou, and Yami. In 2002 indigenous peoples in Taiwan totaled 433,689, with the Amis representing 32.3 percent of the total, followed by the Atayal (14 percent) and the Paiwan (13.8 percent). Many of these indigenous people live in the eastern half of Taiwan on mountainous reservations that cannot be sold to non-aborigines.

Languages: The major and official language is Mandarin Chinese (Kuo-yü, or national language), which is the first language of about 20 percent of the population, mainly in Taipei (Taipei dialect) and other large cities, and is spoken as a second language by many others. The Taiwanese dialect (T'ai-yü, also known as Minnan) is spoken by about 70 percent of the population and is becoming widely used in the broadcast media. Although there are about 4 million Hakka in Taiwan, the Hakka dialect is spoken mostly by the older generation. The Wade-Giles system of romanization of Mandarin Chinese words prevails in Taiwan even though in 1984 the Ministry of Education adopted a modified system of Mandarin romanization called Gwoyeu Romatzyh (National Phonetic Symbols), which was devised by the Republic of China government in 1928. Then, in 2002 the government officially adopted the Tongyong (universal) Pinyin (combined sound) system—similar to Hanyu (Han language) Pinyin used in mainland China—as recommended in 1996 by the Educational Reform Council. Aboriginal peoples once spoke 24 Austronesian languages, but seven of these languages are extinct, with only a few elderly people knowing a few words. The population includes a few thousand Japanese speakers; Japanese is spoken mostly among elderly aboriginal populations and as a second language by Mandarin, Taiwanese, and Hakka speakers.

Religion: Freedom of religion is guaranteed in Article 13 of the Republic of China constitution. In the early 2000s, of Taiwan's 12.7 million temple, church, and mosque members, 42.9 percent were Buddhists, 35.6 percent were adherents of Daoism (Taoism), 6.6 percent were believers in I-kuan Tao (Yiguan Dao, Religion of One Unity, a modern syncretic faith), 4.7 percent were Protestants, and 2.3 percent were Roman Catholics. The 16 other religions tabulated by the Ministry of Interior include Islam (4.1 percent) and Confucianism, described as "a philosophy with a religious function" (1 percent). Taiwan has 23,201 temples and churches, and most are Daoist temples (37 percent), Buddhist temples (17.4 percent), or Protestant churches (15.5 percent). Among the general population, religious beliefs are often eclectic rather than exclusive, such as Christianity and Islam. Many people in Taiwan belong to a particular temple or specific religious sect but engage regularly in religious practices based on one or more religious traditions. Thus, small shrines are seen throughout Taiwan honoring a deity, a hero, or an ancestor. The goddess Mazu, to whom are attributed seeing the future, curing the ill, and rescuing people imperiled on the sea, is extremely popular in Taiwan, and more than 400 temples honor her. While many aborigines are animists whose beliefs center around deities in nature, spirits of dead people, living creatures, and ghosts, more than 70 percent are said to be Christians.

Education and Literacy: The right to an education is guaranteed by the Republic of China constitution. A nine-year compulsory public education system has been in place since 1979, with six years of elementary school and three years of junior high. Nearly 94 percent of junior high graduates go on to senior high or vocational schools. Mandarin Chinese is the medium of instruction. In school year 2003–4, the system included 3,306 preschools, with 240,926 students and 21,251 teachers; 2,638 primary schools, with 1.9 million students and 103,793 teachers; and 1,192 secondary schools, including vocational schools, with 1.7 million students and 97,738 teachers. During the same school year, there were 158 institutions of higher education, with 1.3 million students and 47,472 faculty members, and another 958 special and supplementary schools (such as adult and continuing education), with 5.7 million students and 277,773 teachers. Enrollment rates have improved with the increasing development of Taiwan's economy. In 2002 some 97 percent of children aged 6 to 11 were enrolled in primary schools, and 90 percent of children aged 12 to 17 were enrolled in secondary schools. Some 46 percent of the population was enrolled in tertiary levels of education (vocational schools, colleges, universities, adult education, and other postsecondary schools), and 12.9 students per 100 households were enrolled in colleges and universities in 2002. Graduate programs are expanding in the early twenty-first century, but many college degree holders seeking postgraduate education continue to go abroad. Formerly, the Kuomintang (KMT) imbued the education system with the goal of reunification with China under KMT rule. After the KMT lost control of the executive branch of government to the Democratic Progressive Party (DPP) in 2000, the new school curriculum began to offer more Taiwan-based content, including the study of Taiwanese language and literature. Taiwan had a literacy rate of 96.1 percent as of 2003.

Health: In 2002 Taiwan had nearly 1.6 physicians and 5.9 hospital beds per 1,000 population. Throughout the Taiwan area, there were 36 hospitals and 2,601 clinics in 2002. Per capita health expenditures totaled US$752 in 2000. Health expenditures constituted 5.8 percent of the gross domestic product (GDP) in 2001; 64.9 percent of the expenditures were from public funds. As with other developed economies, Taiwan's people are well-nourished but face such health problems as chronic obesity and heart disease. In 2003 the severe acute respiratory syndrome (SARS) crisis hit Taiwan, but the island was later declared safe by the World Health Organization (WHO). In November 2004, the Department of Health announced that human immunodeficiency virus/acquired immune deficiency syndrome (HIV/AIDS) had become an increasingly serious problem in Taiwan. The first reported case surfaced in 1984. In 2004 there were 6,850 known cases, with 92.9 percent of the infections occurring in Taiwanese and 7.1 percent in foreigners. In 2003 there were 860 new cases of HIV infections, and by October 2004, 1,120 new cases were confirmed on the island. This announcement was followed by the launching of a new public awareness campaign.

Welfare: The government has offered a national health insurance program since 1995 through the National Health Insurance Bureau. Under this plan, employers pay 60 percent of the costs, employees 30 percent, and the government 10 percent. In 1984 the government established rules for the allocation and management of a then-new Workers' Retirement Fund. The rules provide that a retiree is entitled to a maximum pension equal to 45 times his average wage in the six months prior to retirement. To ensure that workers receive this pension should their employer file for bankruptcy, the government also set up a Wage Arrears Repayment Fund to which all employers are required to contribute a small percentage of each employee's salary. Since 1993, a monthly subsidy has been provided to all people 65 and older and to low-income families. In 2002 the government established a monthly pension of US$86 for residents 65 years or older who meet certain requirements.

ECONOMY

Overview: Taiwan is characterized as a "dynamic capitalist" economy. Under the liberalized economic policies in place since the early 1990s, the government has gradually decreased the guidance it provides over investment and foreign trade, as reflected in the privatization of large government-owned banks and industries. Since the 1950s, exports have provided the primary impetus for industrialization. Taiwan evolved from a minor agricultural exporter to the world's largest exporter of computer monitors, a leading personal computer exporter, and a major producer of the world's electronics. Because of its relatively conservative financial approach and its entrepreneurial strengths, Taiwan did not suffer as much as many of its neighbors did from the Asian financial crisis in 1997–98. However, as a result of the turn-of-the-century international economic downturn, along with problems in government policy coordination and bad debts in the banking system, Taiwan went into recession in 2001, the first year of negative growth ever recorded, but experienced moderate recovery in 2002. In January 2002, Taiwan entered the World Trade Organization as a special customs territory. Another major factor in this new growth has been improved economic ties with mainland China, which by 2003 had become Taiwan's largest two-way trading partner.

Gross Domestic Product (GDP)/Gross National Product (GNP): GDP for 2004 was US$313.1 billion, and the GDP growth rate was estimated at 3.2 percent in 2004. GNP in 2004 was US$313.6 billion, with a growth rate of 5.9 percent. Per capita GNP in 2003 was US$13,995. Based on 2004 estimates, Taiwan's purchasing parity power (PPP) was nearly US$528.6 billion total, or US$23,400 per capita.

Government Budget: It is estimated that for 2004, revenues were nearly US$56.7 billion and expenditures US$69.2 billion, including US$14.4 billion in capital expenditures. The central government budget for 2005 was US$48.1 billion.

Inflation: The inflation rate is estimated at –0.3 percent for 2004.

Agriculture, Forestry, and Fishing: Agriculture has played a decreasing role in the economy since the 1960s. Agriculture represented 28.5 percent of the gross domestic product (GDP) in 1960, 4.9 percent in 1987, but only 1.7 percent in 2004, when the sector experienced a –0.1 percent growth rate. The major agricultural products, according to their production volume, are vegetables, sugarcane, rice, fruit, sweet potatoes, corn, peanuts, and tea. Based on the number of head of livestock, most animal husbandry production is of poultry, pigs, sheep and goats, and cattle. Forestry products include industrial wood (about 64 percent of the total and including sawn timber, raw timber, and bamboo polls) and firewood. Overall, forestry is of diminishing importance, and resources are either of low quality or inaccessible. Despite Taiwan's island location, fishing plays a minor role—about 25 percent of total agricultural production—in the economy. In 2003 some 1.1 million tons of fish, 304 tons of shellfish and other aquatic animals—mostly from offshore and deep-sea fishing—and 40,900 tons of aquatic plants were caught or harvested. Taiwan's fishing fleet is composed of around 29,000 boats. Aquaculture provides about 20 percent of Taiwan's seafood production.

Mining and Minerals: The mining sector has been in decline since the 1970s. Minor amounts of clay, copper, dolomite, feldspar, limestone, manganese, marble, salt, serpentine, and sulphur are still extracted. Domestic coal mining fell precipitously after the mid- to late 1960s and is made up for by more economical imports. The last coal mine closed in 2001.

Industry and Manufacturing: Manufacturing is the key to Taiwan's economic success and continues to account for most of the island's exports. However, the sector has been slowly declining as a share of the gross domestic product (GDP) since the late 1980s (when it accounted for 42.9 percent of GDP), as low-technology industries moved elsewhere and value-added services increased. The major industries are electronics—Taiwan is the world's largest producer of computer monitors and one of the world's leading personal computer exporters—as well as petrochemicals, textiles, iron and steel, machinery, cement, and food processing. In 2004 industry registered a 2.9 percent growth rate and produced 29.7 percent of GDP, including manufacturing, which produced 25.7 percent of GDP. Taiwan's information-technology products increasingly—about 63 percent of the total—are manufactured by Taiwan-owned companies in mainland China. Taiwan retains the research and development and high-end product manufacturing (such as semiconductors and liquid crystal display (LCD) monitors) and leaves bulk production to mainland subsidiaries.

Energy: Taiwan depends on foreign supplies for 98 percent of its energy needs. Of the remaining 2 percent produced domestically, more than 50 percent is supplied by 41 hydroelectric plants. Of the energy imports, about 50 percent are of crude oil and petroleum products, 30 percent are coal, and 10 percent are liquefied natural gas, all of which are used to provide fuel to 31 thermal power plants. Taiwan also has three nuclear power plants, which depend on foreign fuel imports. Energy was long the monopoly of the government-owned Taiwan Power (Taipower), but even with deregulation and the beginning of the privatization of Taipower in 2001, as of 2004 only 4 of 11 planned independent power plants had come online. Taipower itself was slated for full privativization in 2005. In 2001 Taiwan produced 151.1 billion kilowatt hours of electric energy and used 140.5 billion kilowatt hours. Its refined oil production totaled an estimated 1,100 barrels per day in 2004 against a consumption (for which 2001 is the latest year reported) of 988,999 barrels per day. Taiwan has proven oil reserves of 2 million barrels. Natural gas production reached 750 million cubic meters in 2001 against a consumption of 6.6 billion cubic meters. Taiwan has 38.2 billion cubic meters of proven natural gas reserves. Although Taiwan's exports of natural gas amounted to 410 million cubic meters in 2001, imports for the same year totaled 6.3 billion cubic meters.

Services: The services sector is Taiwan's largest, producing 68.5 percent of the gross domestic product (GDP), with a 3.1 percent growth rate in 2004. The sector includes finance, insurance and real estate; commerce (trade and eating-drinking places); social, personal, and related community services; transportation, storage, and communications; business services; producers of government services; and other producers. The largest subsector, at 21.2 percent of GDP, was commerce.

Banking and Finance: Taiwan's central bank, the semiautonomous Central Bank of China, was established in 1924, relocated to Taiwan in December 1949, and resumed full operations in 1961. Since 1979, the Central Bank of China has been subordinate to the Executive Yuan but has independent authority in setting monetary policies. As with other sectors of the economy, Taiwan's banking and finance sector has undergone reforms. Since 1989, interest rates have been removed from government control, and restrictions on establishing bank branches were lifted. Investment and trust companies were allowed to become full-fledged banks, new private banks were permitted to open, and state banks were privatized. Structural weaknesses that had negative effects on the financial sector in the late 1990s were the object of further government reform in the early 2000s. These weaknesses included the establishment of too many small and under-capitalized banks and resulting fierce competition among them, lending to too many companies suffering from short-term financial difficulties, and the division of responsibility for governmental regulatory duties. As reform measures, taxes were cut, consolidation and diversification were encouraged, and the government-funded Financial Reconstruction Fund was established. By 2003 Taiwan had 52 private and government-owned banks, and the government planned to divest itself of commercial bank ownership. Taiwan's stock market also is in flux. The oldest and largest stock market is the Taiwan Stock Exchange (Taisdaq), the majority traders (80 percent) in which are retail investors, whose holdings are subject to cross-Taiwan Strait activities, regional economic trends, and increased margin trading. The domestic futures market began in 1998 with the opening of the Taiwan International Mercantile Exchange (Taimex).

Tourism: Tourism is a minor industry in Taiwan but has gradually improved since the late 1980s, when Taiwan was receiving about 1.2 million foreign visitors a year. By 2002 that number had risen to more than 2.9 million but dropped in 2003 to 2.2 million with the outbreak of severe acute respiratory syndrome (SARS). Most visitors in 2003 came from Japan (29 percent) and the United States (12 percent). However, some 19 percent were overseas Chinese from a variety of countries throughout the world who traveled to Taiwan on Taiwan passports. Tourist spending also dropped in 2003, from US$4.5 billion in 2002 to US$2.9 billion in 2003.

Labor: Taiwan's labor force was estimated to number nearly 10.1 million in 2004. Of this total, based on 2001 estimates, 7.5 percent were involved in agriculture, 35 percent in industry, and 57 percent in services. The Chinese Federation of Labor represents 43 national and regional labor union federations, which, in turn, represent some 1 million workers. Other federations include the Taiwan Confederation of Trade Unions and the National Trade Union Confederation. As of 2003, about 29 percent of the labor force belonged to 4,111 registered labor unions. During the recession of 2001, Taiwan experienced the highest unemployment rates in its history (4.5 percent). The unemployment rate was estimated at 4.1 percent as of late 2004.

Foreign Economic Relations: Despite the dearth of diplomatic relations with foreign nations, Taiwan enjoys vigorous international trade relations. Taiwan's phenomenal economic growth has been fueled largely by the export trade, and, thus, Taiwan depends on an open-world trade regime. Since the 1950s, Taiwan has moved from exporting primarily agricultural products to exporting primarily industrial goods, which in 2005 represented 98 percent of all of Taiwan's exports. In January 2002, Taiwan became a member of the World Trade Organization as a special customs territory. Throughout its modernization period, Taiwan's largest trading partner was the United States. However, since 2003 Japan and China both have overtaken the United States in this role. In 2004 Taiwan's total foreign trade amounted to US$341.8 billion. The largest two-way trade partners were Japan (16.6 percent), China (14.8 percent), the United States (14.5 percent), Hong Kong (9.3 percent), and South Korea (4.9 percent).

Imports: In 2004 Taiwan imported a total of US$167.8 billion, principally machinery, electrical equipment, minerals, and precision instruments. The major import partners were Japan (25.9 percent), the United States (12.8 percent), China (9.9 percent), South Korea (6.9 percent), and Germany (3.4 percent).

Exports: In 2004 Taiwan exported a total of US$174 billion, principally computer products, electronic equipment, metals, textiles, plastics and rubber products, and chemicals. The major export partners were China (19.5 percent), Hong Kong (17.1 percent), the United States (16.1 percent), Japan (7.5 percent), and Singapore (6.3 percent).

Trade Balance: Taiwan's exports in 2003 were US$143.4 billion against US$118.5 billion in imports, leaving a positive trade balance of US$24.9 billion. Its largest surplus is with China (more than US$22 billion in 2003), an amount that is likely to decrease when and if the government lifts restrictions on imports of merchandise from the mainland.

Balance of Payments: The current account balance has fluctuated in recent decades. It increased in the years up to 1991 (US$12.5 billion), then went into almost annual declines for the next several years, and bottomed out at US$3.4 billion in 1998. Since then it has improved as exports increased during the same period. Taiwan's current account balance in 2003 was US$29.2 billion and the overall balance was US$37.1 billion.

External Debt: Taiwan's external debt was estimated at US$53.4 billion in 2004, almost entirely private-sector debt. The public debt stood at 30.5 percent of gross domestic product (GDP) in 2004. Taiwan's foreign exchange reserves totaled US$206 billion at the start of 2004, the third largest in the world behind China and Japan.

Foreign Investment: The growth of Taiwan's export trade in the 1990s led to an average growth of 10 percent a year in private-sector investment. But private-sector investment is susceptible to fluctuations in export growth, and when the latter stalled during the 2001 recession, so did capital investment. Taiwan is a net investor overseas. In the 1996–2002 period, Taiwan's overseas investments totaled US$34.4 billion, while foreign direct investment in Taiwan—mostly from Japan and the United States—totaled US$17.8 billion. Most of Taiwan's overseas investments are in the United States (US$4.9 billion, or 18.4 percent of total investments in 1992–2002), followed by those in Southeast Asian nations (US$4.8 billion, or 16.1 percent of total investments during the same period). The Ministry of Economic Affairs is responsible for overseeing government-approved investment in mainland China. Between 1991, when restrictions were lifted, and 2003, the ministry approved more than US$33.6 billion in investments in China, making investment from Taiwan the fifth largest in China. However, others have estimated the actual figure as closer to US$100 billion. Up to 2000, the Kuomintang (KMT) government encouraged a slow and cautious pace in mainland investment, a move that was unpopular with the business community. The Democratic Progressive Party (DPP), which officially did not seek to open direct links with the People's Republic of China, initiated a more open policy, but many investors saw no difference from the KMT policy.

Currency and Exchange Rate: Taiwan's currency is the New Taiwan Dollar (NT$), which was instituted in 1949. The exchange rate in March 2005 was US$1 = NT$30.82. The New Taiwan Dollar is made up of 100 cents. Coins are issued in denominations of NT$0.50, NT$1, NT$10, and NT$50, and banknotes are issued in denominations of NT$100, NT$500, NT$1,000, and NT$2,000.

Fiscal Year: Calendar year, starting in 2001.

TRANSPORTATION AND TELECOMMUNICATIONS

Overview: Taiwan has a modern and comprehensive transportation infrastructure. With two international airports serving the world's major airlines, an extensive network of highways and expressways, and a railroad system that circles the island and is soon to be joined by bullet-train service north to south, the island is well served. Additionally, it has modern port facilities at strategic locations to export its large industrial production. Taiwan's telecommunications are among the most sophisticated and well used in the world.

Roads: Taiwan had 37,342 kilometers of highways, including 608 kilometers of expressways, in 2003. Of the total, about 88 percent of roads were paved and about 12 percent were unpaved rural roads. In 2003 Taiwan had 5.2 million passenger automobiles, 25,600 buses and coaches, 885,780 trucks and goods-carrying vehicles, and 12.4 million motorcycles and motor scooters in use. In the same year, some 388,000 new passenger automobiles and 4,100 new trucks and buses were manufactured.

Railroads: Construction of Taiwan's first railroad began in 1887 and was completed in 1891. That same year, the Taiwan Railway Administration (TRA) was established as a public utility. It now is part of the Ministry of Communications and Transportation. Most other routes were built during the Japanese occupation, between 1908 and 1941. By 2003 Taiwan had 1,103.7 kilometers of 1.067-meter track. Of this total, 519 kilometers were electrified, 514.8 kilometers had double tracks, and 588.9 kilometers had single tracks. The TRA operates commuter, long-distance passenger, and freight services. There are three main lines, the Western and Eastern lines, which join in the north at Chi-lung (Keelung), and the South-Link Line, which was completed in 1991 and connects the southern terminals of the Western and Eastern lines. There also are three branch lines. At the start of 2004, the TRA had 173 electric and 155 diesel locomotives, 171 diesel multiple-unit railcars, 66 diesel single-unit railcars, 563 electric multiple-unit railcars, 1,351 passenger coaches, and 2,755 freight cars. Daily, the TRA system carries nearly 500,000 passengers and about 50,000 tons of freight. During 2003 railroads carried 478.2 million passengers, accounting for nearly 11.2 billion passenger/kilometers, and 16.7 million tons of freight, accounting for 863.9 million ton/kilometers. The Taiwan High Speed Rail Corporation has completed construction of double-track, standard-gauge bullet-train service between Taipei and Kao-hsiung. When fully operational and using Japanese-made Shinkansen trains, it will take 90 minutes to travel the 345-kilometer route at 350 kilometers per hour. In January 2005, the eight-station (four other stations are planned) route was undergoing running tests, and operations are expected to begin in fall 2005. Another 1,400 kilometers of 0.762-meter narrow-gauge track belong to the Taiwan Sugar Corporation and the Taiwan Forestry Bureau and are used primarily to transport their products and a limited number of passengers.

Rapid Transit: Construction of the Taipei Rapid Transit System, or Metro Taipei, began in 1987. The first line, the elevated Muzha Line, went into operation in 1996, and between 1997 and 2004 four additional lines and three branch lines became operational. The 65.3 kilometers of lines in operation have 68 stations and a combination of underground, elevated, and surface tracks. Four underground or elevated lines are under construction, with opening dates between 2007 and 2010, either as extensions or branches of existing lines. Three other lines are planned. The two-line, 42.7-kilometer-long, 37-station Kao-hsiung Mass Rapid Transit system has been under construction since 2001. The mostly underground system is scheduled for completion in late 2006. Proposals have been made for similar systems in T'ai-chung and T'ai-nan.

Ports: Taiwan has five major international ports. The largest facility, according to cargo volume, is Kao-hsiung, which is located in southwestern Taiwan and handles more than 50 percent of the total. It is one of the busiest ports in the world. Other international ports are An-p'ing, north of Kao-hsiung; Chi-lung (Keelung), on the northern tip of Taiwan; Hua-lien, on the central east coast; Su-ao, an auxiliary port to Chi-lung; and T'ai-chung, on the central west coast, about 25 kilometers west of the city of T'ai-chung. Taiwan's merchant fleet has some 649 vessels, including 130 ships of 1,000 gross registered tons or more. This latter category includes 36 bulk carriers, 23 cargo ships, 2 chemical tankers, 3 combination bulk carriers, 37 container ships, 17 petroleum tankers, 10 refrigerated cargo ships, and 2 roll on/roll off ships. In 2003 some 457 Taiwanese-owned ships were registered in other countries.

Inland and Coastal Waterways: Taiwan has no significant inland waterways. Its coastal waterways are served by numerous small, medium, and large ports.

Civil Aviation and Airports: Taiwan has 40 airports, 37 of which have paved runways, and three heliports. Of paved-runway airports, eight have runways of more than 3,047 meters. Taiwan has two international airports. Chiang Kai-shek International Airport, located at T'ao-yüan, 40 kilometers west of Taipei, opened in 1979 and was expanded in 2000. It has two terminals serving 32 domestic and foreign airlines; its longest runway is 3,600 meters. The other is the Kao-hsiung International Airport, 10 kilometers outside of Kao-hsiung. The airport's longest runway is 3,150 meters, and its international terminal was completed in 1997. Taiwan's China Airlines (CAL) is the major domestic and international carrier. CAL has a fleet of 55 Airbus and Boeing aircraft and 22 more on order from the same two companies. As with many state-owned companies, CAL has been undergoing privatization. Other major carriers are EVA Airways, Far Eastern Air Transport, Mandarin Airlines, Transasia Airways, and UNI Airways, with fleets of aircraft serving a variety of regional and domestic destinations. In 2003 civil aviation transported 37.8 million passengers and 1.6 million tons of freight to, from, and within Taiwan.

Pipelines: Taiwan had 25 kilometers of condensate pipelines and 435 kilometers of gas pipelines in 2004.

Telecommunications: Taiwan had 135 AM radio stations, 49 FM stations, and some 16 million radios reported in operation in 2002. Many stations also offered Internet access to their broadcasts. In 1997 there were 29 television broadcast stations. Almost every household in Taiwan has a color television (99.6 sets per 100 households, or around 7 million sets, in 2002) and many also have cable service (74.8 cable receivers per 100 households in 2002). In 2003 there were nearly 13.4 main-line telephones, and in 2004 there were more than 23 million cellular telephone subscribers. The domestic telephone system is fully digital. International service is provided via two earth satellite stations servicing two Intelsat satellites, one over the Pacific Ocean and one over the Indian Ocean. Submarine cables connect Taiwan to Japan via Okinawa, Philippines, Guam, Singapore, Hong Kong, Indonesia, Australia, the Middle East, and Western Europe. Taiwanese are major users of the Internet, having more than 7.8 million users in 2003. The Directorate General of Telecommunications, which serves as the telecommunications regulatory authority and determines power and frequencies in Taiwan, is subordinate to the Ministry of Transportation and Communications. The Government Information Office supervises the operation of all radio and television stations, both private and government-owned.

GOVERNMENT AND POLITICS

Government Overview: Taiwan has a multiparty democratic regime headed by a popularly elected president and unicameral legislature in which four major parties maintain two alliances in a new era of coalition politics and divided government. The current governmental system was established by the 1946 constitution of the Republic of China. As envisioned by its founder, Sun Yat-sen (1866–1925), the government has five branches, or *yuans*: executive, legislative, judicial, examination, and control. In March 2004, incumbent President Chen Shui-bian of the Democratic Progressive Party (Minzhu Jinpu Dang, abbreviated as Minjindang; DPP) barely won reelection. In the December 2004 Legislative Yuan elections, Chen's party won the most seats, but the Kuomintang (KMT) increased its tally of seats and, through an alliance with two other parties—the Pan-Blue alliance—could outvote the Chen's Pan-Green alliance. It is thus difficult for the DPP government to further its economic and political reform agendas. In keeping with its trend toward independence, the DPP administration increasingly eschews the Republic of China name.

Taiwan's constitution—that of the Republic of China—was adopted by the National Constituent Assembly in Nanjing, China, on December 25, 1946. It was promulgated on January 1, 1947, and took effect on December 25, 1947. On April 18, 1948, the National Assembly added to the constitution a set of "Temporary Provisions Effective During the Period of Communist Rebellion," which in effect superseded the constitution and gave the president emergency powers. These provisions were in effect until terminated in 1991. To bring the constitution into line with Taiwan's new situation, in 1991 the National Assembly passed the first amendment to the 1946 constitution. It has 10 articles, including provision for regular elections for the Legislative Yuan and the National Assembly; authorization for the president to issue emergency decrees to avert imminent danger to the security of the nation or of the people; and the stipulation that rights and obligations between people on both sides of the Taiwan Strait may be regulated by law. Since then the constitution has been amended five more times, in 1992, 1994, 1997, 1999 (voided in 2000), and 2000 (revised the fourth amendment articles), all aimed at fostering constitutional democracy. The constitution now has 175 articles in 9 chapters, with 6 amendments (4 of which are operative) and 11 operative "additional articles." The constitution invokes the Three Principles of the People (Sun Yat-sun's *San Min Chu I*—nationalism, democracy, and social well-being). Article 1 describes the Republic of China as a "democratic republic of the people, by the people, and for the people."

Executive Branch: The chief of state on Taiwan since May 20, 2000, and reelected in March 2004, is President Chen Shui-bian. The vice president is Lu Hsiu-lien (Annette Lu), Chen's running mate in 2000 and 2004. The government is led by a cabinet known as the Executive Yuan, which is the highest administrative organ and is responsible to the Legislative Yuan. The head of government (or premier) is the president of the Executive Yuan, Hsieh Chang-ting (Frank Hsieh, since February 2005), who is assisted by a vice premier (Wu Rong-I, since February 2005). The premier is appointed by the president; vice premiers are appointed by the president on the recommendation of the premier. In February 2005, the Executive Yuan had 45 members, including the premier, vice premier, secretary general, 38 individuals holding the title of minister or minister without portfolio, 8 commission and council chairs, the governor of the Central Bank of China, and the director of the National Palace Museum.

Legislative Branch: Taiwan has two unicameral legislative bodies. The highest legislative organ in Taiwan is the Legislative Yuan. It has 225 members elected for three-year terms, and incumbents are eligible for reelection. Of the total seat holders, 168 are elected by popular vote, 41 are elected on the basis of the proportion of island-wide votes received by the participating political parties, 8 are elected from overseas Chinese constituencies on the basis of island-wide votes received by participating parties, and 8 are elected by popular vote among the aboriginal populations. The number of seats in the Legislative Yuan is scheduled to be reduced from 225 to 113 with the election of 2007. The president of the Executive Yuan in February 2005 was Wang Jin-pyng.

The other unicameral legislative body is the National Assembly. Once a powerful body that elected the chief of state, the National Assembly has been weakened by means of various constitutional amendments between 1991 and 2000. It became a 300-seat, non-standing body with delegates nominated by political parties on the basis of proportional representation within three months of a Legislative Yuan call to amend the constitution, impeach the president, or change national borders. Most of its original functions, including hearing the president's state of the nation address and approving the president's nominations of members of the Council of Grand Justices and the heads of the Examination Yuan and Control Yuan, have been transferred to the Legislative Yuan.

Judicial Branch: The Judicial Yuan is composed of justices appointed by the president with the consent of the Legislative Yuan. The Council of Grand Justices, the main body of the Judicial Yuan, comprises the president (in February 2005, Weng Yueh-sheng) and vice president of the Judicial Yuan, who serve for four-year terms, and 13 other grand justices who serve for eight years. The council interprets the constitution and "unifies the interpretation of laws and ordinances." The Judicial Yuan is in charge of civil, criminal, and administrative cases. It also deals with cases concerning the discipline of public officials. Its subordinate organs are the Supreme Court (with 8 civil and 12 criminal divisions); high courts (currently, there is one court serving Taiwan and P'eng-hu, with branch courts in T'ai-chung, T'ai-nan, Kao-hsiung, and Hua-lien, which addresses civil, criminal, juvenile, traffic, and labor cases); district courts (20, each with civil, criminal, and summary divisions); the Supreme Administrative Court; high administrative courts (three, which, together with the Supreme Administrative Court, are part of a "two-level and two-instance system" for administrative litigation established in 2000); and the Commission on the Disciplinary Sanctions of Functionaries, which exercises jurisdiction over cases brought before the Control Yuan. In the early 2000s, the Judicial Yuan has endeavored to reduce political influence on judges. An independent committee using secret ballots now decides judicial appointments and promotions. Except in the case of decisions by assistant judges, judicial decisions are no longer subject to review by presiding judges.

Examination Yuan: The Examination Yuan is the fourth branch of government. It has a president (in February 2005, Yao Chia-wen) and 19 members, all of whom were appointed in 2002 for six-year terms by the president, with the approval of the Legislative Yuan. The Examination Yuan Council is made up of the Examination Yuan president and vice president and one other member. The council makes policy and decides all significant matters within the jurisdiction of the Examination Yuan, that is, examinations, pay, conditions of employment, and training. The Examination Yuan also oversees the civil service pension fund. Its subordinate bodies are the Ministry of Examination, the Ministry of Civil Service, the Civil Service Protection and Training Commission, and the Supervisory Board of the Public Service Pension Fund. The Examination Yuan also supervises the operations of the Central Personnel Administration, which was established under the Executive Yuan in 1967.

Control Yuan: The Control Yuan is the fifth branch of government. It meets monthly with its president (in February 2005, Fredrick Chien; Chien Fu) serving as chair. The Control Yuan has seven committees, which handle cases on domestic and ethnic minority affairs; foreign and overseas Chinese affairs; national defense and intelligence affairs; finance and economic affairs; education and cultural affairs; transportation, communications, and procurement affairs; and judicial affairs and prison administration. It has a supervisory role with respect to security matters, censure, and audit. The Control Yuan also has the authority to impeach public officials at the central and local levels. It once was a parliamentary body with 223 members, but after being reformed into a quasi-judicial branch of government in 1992, its membership dropped to 29. Although the Control Yuan once had the power to impeach the president and vice president, a constitutional amendment moved that function to the Legislative Yuan in 2000.

Administrative Divisions: Taiwan has two provincial-level units: the Taiwan Provincial Government, which administers Taiwan and the P'eng-hu Islands (Pescadores, 64 islands), and the Fu-chien Provincial Government, which has control of some 20 offshore islands formerly appertaining to the mainland's Fujian Province.

Provincial and Local Government: The Taiwan Provincial Government has jurisdiction over the island of Taiwan and the P'eng-hu Islands (Pescadores). The governor of Taiwan Province presides over a 19-member Taiwan Provincial Consultative Council. There also is a popularly elected Taiwan Provincial Assembly. Taiwan Province is subdivided into 16 counties (*hsien*), headed by magistrates; 5 municipalities (*shih*), headed by mayors; and 2 special municipalities (*chuan-shih*)—Taipei and Kao-hsiung, also headed by mayors. However, Taipei and Kao-hsiung and all of Taiwan's counties and cities are directly administered by the Executive Yuan. The capital of Taiwan Province since 1989 has been Chung-hsing-hsin-ts'un (Chung-hsing New Village) in Nan-t'ou County. The Republic of China also has administrative control over two counties subordinate to the Fu-chien Provincial Government: Kinmen and Lienchiang counties. Kinmen County includes the island of Kinmen and other outlying islands, which are offshore from the mainland city of Xiamen (Hsia-men or Amoy). The part of Lienchiang County controlled by the Taiwan authorities includes Matsu and its outlying islands. It is to the north of Kinmen, offshore from the mouth of the mainland's Minjiang (Min River) and the provincial capital of Fuzhou. From 1956 to 1992, the armed forces had full administrative control of Kinmen and Lienchiang. In 1992 local autonomy was restored to both counties as part of the constitutional reforms, giving their residents the same rights and freedoms as all people in Taiwan. The Fu-chien Provincial Consultative Council, presided over by the governor of Fu-chien, has offices in the town of Kinmen on Kinmen Island (Chin-men Tao). Throughout Taiwan, P'eng-hu, and the Fu-chien islands there are popularly elected county and municipal assemblies and village and town councils.

Judicial and Legal System: The legal code is based on the German-based civil-law system that was brought to Taiwan by the Kuomintang government after World War II. The current legal system used throughout Taiwan is derived from the national constitution, civil laws enacted by the legislature, and the Code of Civil Procedure, all of which are applied through the three-tier court system (district courts and their branches, which hear civil and criminal cases; high courts and their branches, which hear appeals against judgments of district courts or their branches; and the Supreme Court at the highest appellate level). Judges are given life-time appointments but can be removed if found guilty of a criminal offense, subjected to disciplinary measure, or declared to be under interdiction.

Electoral System: Article 129 of the constitution guarantees universal, equal, and direct suffrage by secret ballot. Persons who have reached age 20 can vote, and persons 23 years and older can run for office. Article 129 of the constitution provides for presidential and vice presidential candidates running on the same ticket and elected by popular vote to four-year terms. The next Legislative Yuan election will be held in December 2007 and the next presidential election, in March 2008. In elections for special municipality mayors, county magistrates, provincial-level municipality mayors, rural and urban township magistrates, and county-level city mayors, each voter casts one vote in a single-member district, and the candidate who receives a plurality of the votes is elected. Elections for the Legislative Yuan, special municipal councils, county or city councils, and township councils use the single, non-transferable vote method. Normally, several representatives are elected from a single electoral district based on existing administrative boundaries. Each voter casts one vote, and several leading candidates are elected. Prior to an election, each party submits two lists of candidates, one for the national constituency and the other for overseas Chinese communities. Voters do not vote directly for candidates on the party lists. Instead, they vote in their respective single, non-transferable-vote districts, and the votes obtained by all candidates are totaled according to party affiliation. The seats for the national constituency and overseas Chinese communities are then distributed proportionally among the parties that get at least 5 percent of total valid votes nationwide. National and local elections are held and supervised by the Central Elections Commission, an organization subordinate to the Executive Yuan. Article 133 of the constitution provides for recall of a duly elected candidate, and Article 136 provides for initiatives and referenda.

Politics and Political Parties: After years of dominance by the Kuomintang (Nationalist Party), from 1949 to 1989, Taiwan developed a multiparty democracy from among splinters of the Kuomintang as well as opposition groups. The most successful party in this new era is the Democratic Progressive Party (Minzhu Jinpu Dang, abbreviated as Minjindang; DPP), which has had successes in the Legislative Yuan elections since its establishment in 1986. Its candidate, Chen Shui-bian, won the presidency in 2000 and 2004. In the March 20, 2004, Chen and his running mate, Vice President Lu Hsiu-lien (Annette Lu), garnered 50.1 percent of the popular votes while their opponents, Lien Chan of the Kuomintang (KMT, or Nationalist Party) and his vice presidential running mate, James C.Y. Soong of the People First Party (Qinmindang, a KMT breakaway party, PFP), won 49.9 percent. In the December 11, 2004, Legislative Yuan elections, the DPP won 36 percent of the vote (89 seats) to the Kuomintang's 33 percent (79 seats). The other parties of note were the PFP, which won 14 percent of the vote (34 seats), and the Taiwan Solidarity Union (Taiwan Tuanjie Lianmeng; TSU), which took 8 percent of the vote (12 seats). The Non-Partisan Solidarity Union (Wudang Tuanjie Lianmeng, which won 6 seats), the New Party (Hsin Tang or Xindang, formerly the Chinese New Party, Zhongguo Xindang, which won 1 seat), and independents (non-party—*tang-wai* or *dangwai*, 4 seats) hold the other 11

Legislative Yuan seats. Four major parties form two alliances: the pro-independence Pan-Green alliance includes the DPP and the TSU. The pro-reunification Pan-Blue alliance includes the KMT, the PFP, and the New Party. The Pan-Blue alliance holds a slight majority (113 to 102) in the Legislative Yuan. The Non-Partisan Solidarity Union belongs to neither alliance and takes no position on independence.

Mass Media: Taiwan has 841 registered news agencies. The largest is the Central News Agency (CNA), which since 1996 has been a publicly owned, independently run national company organized under government statute. It has 12 domestic and 30 overseas offices and offers Chinese, English, French, and Spanish language news services via radio, television, and the Internet. Once martial law was lifted in 1986, Taiwan's media industry became free from government censorship and other constraints. The three largest daily newspapers, listed according to the size of their circulation, are *Tzu-yu shih-pao* (Liberty Times), *Chung-kuo shih-pao* (China Times), and *Lien-ho pao* (United Daily News), each of which also owns companies that sell other publications, including English-language titles. There is also a government-affiliated newspaper, *Chung-yang jih-pao* (Central Daily News). A daily tabloid, *P'ing-guo jih-pao* (Apple Daily), and a controversial Hong Kong-based weekly tabloid, *I Chou K'an* (One Weekly, which is published in Taiwan with the English subtitle *Next Taiwan*), entered the major newspaper market in 2003 and 2002, respectively, and have achieved wide popular readerships. Taiwan has 598 other newspapers, plus more than 8,000 weekly, biweekly, and monthly magazines. There are more than 7,800 publishing companies in Taiwan, which, in 2001, published a total of 40,235 book titles.

Taiwan's national radio statio is the Central Broadcasting System, which operates Mandarin local variety and news and dialect networks. Radio Taipei International and the Voice of Asia broadcast in 12 foreign languages. Prior to 1993, Taiwan had only 33 radio broadcasting companies. Ten years later, the number had increased to 154, and 20 more were being developed, while 3,217 radio program production companies were registered. Radio stations offer a range of domestic programming in Mandarin, Taiwanese, and Hakka and daily international programming in a variety of Chinese dialects aimed at the mainland and overseas Chinese, as well as Arabic, Indonesian, Japanese, Korean, Mongolian, Thai, Tibetan, Vietnamese, and a number of European languages. By 2004 Taiwan had 63 cable television companies and 132 satellite broadcasting companies in operation.

In 1999 the Legislative Yuan abolished the Publications Law, which the police had used to seize or ban printed material that was considered seditious, treasonous, sacrilegious, interfered with the lawful exercise of public functions, or violated public order or morals. In 2003 the Legislative Yuan approved legislation that barred the government, political parties, and party officials from owning or running media organizations. The law also required that the government and political parties divest themselves of ownership of all television and radio broadcast companies within two years and that officials resign from boards and managerial positions in media companies within six months.

Foreign Relations: Taiwan, as the Republic of China, has formal diplomatic relations with 24 nations and the Holy See. Most of these nations are in Latin America and the Caribbean (12) and Africa (7), as well as several small Pacific Ocean island nations (5). Nations wanting to establish relations with the People's Republic of China have had to first agree to break off relations with the Republic of China. However, to ensure a continuation of representation, nonofficial Taiwan offices handling commercial and cultural relations are maintained by 92 representative offices or branch offices in the capitals and major cities of 59 nations. Reciprocally, 48 nations that do not have official diplomatic relations with Taipei have established 58 representative offices or visa-issuing centers in Taiwan. These offices perform most of the functions of embassies and consulates general.

Relations between Taiwan and the United States are conducted under the framework of three documents. The first is the 1979 U.S. Taiwan Relations Act, which established the legal basis for unofficial relations with Taiwan and which has received reaffirmation from each U.S. administration since its enactment. The second is the 1982 U.S.-China joint communiqué, in which the United States declared it did not intend to seek a long-term policy of arms sales to Taiwan; that its arms sales to Taiwan "would not exceed, either in qualitative or in quantitative terms, the level of those supplied in recent years"; and that it planned to gradually reduce its arms sales to Taiwan. In the same document, China said it would strive for a peaceful resolution of the Taiwan question. The third document is the 1994 U.S. Taiwan Policy Review, in which, while declaring adherence to previous U.S.-China communiqués and the "one China policy," the Clinton Administration said that in view of the changing circumstances in China and Taiwan, the United States would allow top Taiwan leaders to transit the United States, initiate sub-cabinet-level economic dialogue with Taiwan, support Taiwan's membership in international organizations that accept non-state members, and allow high-level U.S. government officials to meet with Taiwan counterparts in unofficial settings and to travel to Taiwan.

Even though Washington terminated its 1954 mutual security treaty with Taiwan in 1979, it has continued to sell defensive military equipment to Taiwan. The United States has repeatedly expressed concern over any coercive measures that Beijing takes or threatens to take against Taiwan and that may contribute to regional instability. In Washington's view, providing defensive weapons to and maintaining unofficial relations with Taiwan are a fundamental part of the U.S. policy that there is but one China and that Taiwan is a part of China. The United States has welcomed and encouraged cross-strait dialogue to reduce tensions and to create an environment for a peaceful resolution of differences between Taiwan and the People's Republic. The United States does not support Taiwan independence and has stated that it is opposed to any attempt by either side to unilaterally alter the status quo in the Taiwan Strait. Taiwan maintains its diplomatic presence in the United States with the Taipei Economic and Cultural Representative Office, which has its headquarters in Taipei and offices in Washington, D.C., and 12 other U.S. cities. The United States reciprocates with its American Institute in Taiwan, with headquarters in Arlington, Virginia, and offices in Taipei and Kao-hsiung.

Relations with Japan and South Korea also are very important. Both are major trading partners and have had long histories of political and cultural exchanges with Taiwan. Both Taiwan and U.S. policy makers see Taiwan, along with Japan and South Korea, as part of the strategic triangle of Asian democratic countries that help promote peace in the Asian-Pacific region.

Taiwan has long maintained close relations with West European nations, with emphasis on trade, cultural, technological, educational, and tourism exchanges. Relations with Europe are conducted both bilaterally and with European institutions, especially the European Union (EU). Taiwan has an embassy at the Holy See and representative offices in the capitals of 19 EU members, as well as in Norway and Switzerland. The Taipei Representative Office in Belgium is in charge of EU affairs. The EU and 18 European nations have representative offices in Taipei.

Cross-Strait Relations: The People's Republic of China considers Taiwan one of its provinces and an inalienable part of China that has been separated from the motherland since 1949. The Republic of China government also holds to the principle that Taiwan is part of China, and reunification and "return to the mainland" are long-held goals. Taipei also has taken the stance that genuine democratization of the mainland is a prerequisite for reunification. While Beijing adamantly opposes independence or any quasi-state status for Taiwan and periodically threatens forceful reunification, Taiwan's leaders have increasingly moved toward de facto independence and rejection of Beijing's proffered "one country, two systems" approach that has been applied to Hong Kong and Macau. Taiwan holds that the two sides of the Taiwan Strait have been governed since 1949 as separate territories and have developed separate identities.

The two sides have had no direct official contact since 1949. At the onset of the reform era on the mainland in 1979, Beijing began making intensive overtures to Taiwan, but Taipei responded with its "three no's policy" (no contacts, no negotiations, and no compromise). However, starting in the early 1980s, both sides allowed economic and trade exchanges, education exchanges, travel, tourism, and other activities. Private exchanges between relatives on the two sides began in 1987. In May 1991, President Lee Teng-hui announced the termination of the "Period of National Mobilization for Suppression of the Communist Rebellion," thereby abandoning the claim to govern mainland China, acknowledging that the Chinese Communist Party regime controls the mainland, and establishing the position that the two sides of the Taiwan Strait are under separate rule. Between 1990 and 1991, Taiwan set up three organizations to administer relations between itself and mainland China. They are the National Unification Council, an advisory board to the president that drafted guidelines in February 1991 calling for a phased approach toward unification; the Mainland Affairs Council, a cabinet-level administrative agency responsible for the overall planning, coordination, evaluation, and implementation of the government's mainland policies; and the Straits Exchange Foundation, a private organization authorized by the government to handle technical and business matters with China. The Act Governing Relations Between Peoples of the Taiwan Area and the Mainland Area was promulgated in 1992 and amended several times since to keep adapting to rapidly changing cross-strait relations. In 1993 representatives from the Straits Exchange Foundation met in Singapore with their mainland counterparts, the representatives of the Association for Relations Across the Taiwan Strait, for the first cross-strait talks in more than 40 years. Beijing's extreme displeasure with the 1995 visit to the United States by Taiwan President Lee Tung-hui and China's 1996 test firing of a guided missile off Taiwan's coast during the campaign for the island's first popularly elected president kept other cross-strait meetings from occurring. The second round of talks between the Straits Exchange Foundation and the Association for Relations Across the Taiwan Strait was held in Shanghai in 1998, and agreement was reached on expanding exchanges. However, when Lee Tung-hui said in a July 1999 interview that a "special state-to-state relationship" existed between Taiwan and China, Beijing suspended further negotiations and has since excoriated Lee.

Despite its great displeasure over Lee Tung-hui's 1999 remarks, Beijing continues to favor the traditional position and policies of the KMT and was very unhappy with the election of a Taiwan independence advocate, Democratic Progressive Party (DPP) candidate Chen Shui-bian, in March 2000. In his inaugural address, Chen tempered his party's outspoken position on independence with the pronouncement of the "five nos," saying that as long as Beijing had no intention of using military force against Taiwan, he would not declare independence, change the name of the nation, push for the inclusion of the "state-to-state" description in the constitution, or promote a referendum on the issue of independence or unification. The "five no's" have been reaffirmed on several occasions since then, including a Lunar News Message on February 24, 2005. Chen also has insisted that the cross-strait dialogue should be conducted without any preconditions, while Beijing insists on recognition of the "one China" concept as a prerequisite, which Chen, while acknowledging this insistence, has stopped short of endorsing. Thereafter, additional progress was made in cross-strait activities, including opening direct transportation, postal services, and trade between China and Kinmen and Matsu; expanding the functions and scope of offshore shipping centers; and opening Taiwan to tourism by mainland citizens. Taiwan's earlier "no haste, be patient" policy regarding direct investment on the mainland was replaced by the principle of "proactive liberalization with effective management."

In the ensuing years, there was little Taiwan could do to assuage Beijing's political concerns, especially following statements such as Chen made in July 2002, characterizing the status quo across the Taiwan Strait as "Taiwan and China standing on opposite sides of the Strait, there is one country on each side." A breakthrough came in 2003, when the two sides agreed to allow indirect chartered air flights from Taiwan on festival holidays, although only the Lunar New Year flights ultimately took place. A further breakthrough was made in January 2005, when Beijing agreed to two-way, round-trip, and direct non-stop charter flights across the Taiwan Strait. The first flights took place on January 29, 2005. In March 2005, China passed a new Taiwan anti-secession law. The law states that China would "never forswear the use of force . . . [and] non-peaceful means . . . would be our last resort when all our efforts for a peaceful reunification should prove futile." Taiwan Premier Frank Hsieh, at a rally in Taipei protesting the new law, said that cross-strait relations were not and never will be a domestic issue as Beijing claims. Pro-independence demonstrators condemned the law and burned People's Republic of China flags in protest.

International Memberships: The Republic of China was one of the founding members of the United Nations (UN) in 1946 and was a permanent member of the UN Security Council. However, following the vote of the UN General Assembly in 1971, China's seat was given to the People's Republic of China, and Taipei's representatives were ousted. Taiwan has campaigned unsuccessfully since 1993 for membership in the UN system and since 1997 for observer status in the World Health Organization. Taiwan belongs to the following multilateral organizations in which statehood is not a requirement for membership: Asia Pacific Economic Cooperation, Asian Development Bank, Central American Bank for Economic Integration, International Chamber of Commerce, International Confederation of Free Trade Unions (ICFTU), International Olympic Committee, World Confederation of Labor, and World Trade Organization (both China and Taiwan became members on January 1, 2002). Although no longer a member of the International Labour Organization (ILO), representatives of Taiwan's Chinese Federation of Labor attend ILO annual meetings as an affiliate of the ICFTU.

Major International Treaties: Treaties signed on behalf of China before 1949 are applicable only to the Republic of China on Taiwan. Because of its international status, Taiwan is not a party to any international environmental agreements. In 1972 Taiwan signed the Biological and Toxin Weapons Convention, but its signature was not recognized because Taiwan is not a sovereign state. Taiwan was not allowed to sign the Chemical Weapons Convention when it came into force in 1997. However, Taiwan has said it will adhere to both of these conventions as well as to the Missile Technology Control Regime.

NATIONAL SECURITY

Armed Forces Overview: The president of the Republic of China is the commander in chief of the armed forces. The Ministry of Defense has various administrative and planning departments. The chief of the general staff oversees military operations through the army, navy, and air force general headquarters, each of which is led by its own commander in chief. The armed forces totaled about 290,000 personnel in 2004. Components are the army (approximately 200,000); navy (45,000), including a marine component (15,000); and air force (45,000). The active military structure is supported by a 1.6 million-strong Reserve Command, of which 1.5 million are army, 32,000 navy, 35,000 marines, and 90,000 air force personnel.

Foreign Military Relations: The United States is Taiwan's most important source of military matériel and supports Taiwan with sales of defensive weaponry necessary to offset an attack from the People's Republic of China.

External Threat: The major threat perceived by Taiwan is from the People's Republic of China, which has periodically and emphatically stated that it will take control of Taiwan by force if necessary.

Defense Budget: Taiwan's annual military expenditures in 2003 totaled US$6.6 billion, or US$293 per capita, almost 2.4 percent of gross domestic product (GDP). The defense budget for 2005 represented 15.4 percent of the total government budget.

Major Military Units: The army has 3 army corps, an airborne special operations command, 10 infantry divisions, 2 mechanized infantry divisions, 3 mobile divisions, 2 air defense brigades, 6 independent armored brigades, 1 tank group, 2 air defense surface-to-air missile groups, 2 aviation groups, and 2 aviation brigades. Three offshore commands, with some 50,000 troops, are located on Kinmen, Matsu, and P'eng-hu islands. The navy is divided into three naval districts, with a headquarters base at Tsoying (north of Kao-hsiung) and bases at An-ping, Hsin-c'hu, Hua-lien, Chi-lung, Kenting, Ma-kung (P'eng-hu Islands), Suao, Tamshui, and Wuchi. Naval aviation units are based at Hua-lien, P'ing-t'ung, and Tsoying. The air force has 13 main air bases and has access to 21 civilian and military airports located throughout the country. The air force is organized into 34 combat, reconnaissance, airborne early warning, electronic warfare, search and rescue, transport, and helicopter squadrons. In 2004 Taiwan set up its new Missile Command under the Army General headquarters. It combines army air-defense missile units and navy antiship, land-based missile units (but not air force land-based missile units).

Major Military Equipment: The army's major military equipment includes 300 main battle tanks, 230 light tanks, 650 armored personnel carriers, 997 pieces of towed artillery, 415 pieces of self-propelled artillery, coastal artillery pieces, more than 300 multiple rocket launchers, mortars, 240 surface-to-surface rockets and missiles, 1,000 antitank guided weapons, more than 500 recoilless launchers, and 400 air defense guns. The navy has 4 submarines, 11 destroyers, 21 frigates, 10 corvettes, 11 large patrol craft, 116 or more fast attack craft (missile), 4 ocean minesweepers, 12 coastal minesweepers, 3 land ships (dock), 18 land ships (tank) and landing ships (medium), 18 landing ships (craft utility), 1 survey ship, 1 combat survey ship, 1 repair ship, 5 or more transport ships, 3 or more salvage ships, and 2 support tankers. The naval aviation wing has shipborne and land-based helicopters and fixed-wing aircraft. The air force has 479 combat aircraft, including 3 fighter squadrons and 20 fighter and ground attack squadrons. The air inventory also includes various reconnaissance aircraft, electronic warfare aircraft, 4 airborne early warning aircraft, 1 squadron of search and rescue aircraft, 3 transport squadrons, 18 helicopters (but no armed helicopters), and 78 training aircraft, as well as a substantial number of air-to-surface, antiradiation, and air-to-air missiles.

Military Service: All males in good health when reaching 18 years of age are liable for 2 years of military service (2 months of basic training followed by 22 months of active duty). Individuals can be drafted as members of the armed forces between ages 19 and 45. National Guard service can substitute for active-duty armed forces service under certain conditions (for example, "average health," poor economic status, or only son of parents more than 70 years of age).

Paramilitary Forces: The Coast Guard has about 22,000 members, mostly involved in guard duty in the Nan-sha (Spratly) and Tung-sha (Pratas) islands. They are organized into 8 local coast guard commands and 25 coast guard battalions. The Customs Service under the Ministry of Finance has about 650 armed officers. There also are 1,000 members of the Maritime Police, with about 38 armed patrol boats. Additionally, about 25,000 personnel belong to security groups under the National Police Administration, Ministry of Interior; Bureau of Investigation, Ministry of Justice; and Military Police, Ministry of Defense.

Foreign Military Forces: The Singapore armed forces have three training camps (for infantry, artillery, and armored forces) in Taiwan. In 2002–4 there was discussion by Singapore about possibly moving some or all of these facilities to China's Hainan Island.

Police and Internal Security: The National Police Administration (NPA) of the Ministry of Interior, the NPA's Criminal Investigation Bureau, and the Ministry of Justice's Investigation Bureau are responsible for law enforcement relating to internal security. The NPA handles national police administrative affairs and commands and supervises all police agencies in Taiwan. The subordinate organizations of the NPA include the Immigration Office, which handles international entries and exits; the Criminal Investigation Police, which is responsible for crime prevention and investigation; the National Highway Police, which maintains traffic order and safety and investigates traffic accidents on national freeways; the Aviation Police, which is in charge of air terminal and airport security; the Railway Police, which maintains railway security; the Taiwan Police College, which is in charge of police education; the Special Police, organized into six headquarters and responsible for guarding central government agencies, assisting with local security, protecting designated organizations, and enforcing security checks at airports; Special Police Provincial Headquarters, which is in charge of security for state-run industries; the National Parks Police Corps, which maintains security, order, and rescue work within national parks; the Aerial Police Brigade, which provides air mobilization support for other police forces; and the Chi-lung (Keelung), Hua-lien, Kao-hsiung, and T'ai-chung harbor police.

Terrorism: Taiwan has not been the target of international terrorist activities but has made preparations to safeguard itself against possible attacks. Following the September 11, 2001, terrorist attacks on the United States, Taiwan increased its own antiterrorist security and that of foreign entities in Taiwan, especially the United States. These measures include more police protection of foreign embassies, representative offices, and related organizations and the exchange of intelligence and information relative to security inspection, anti-money laundering, and energy security. The government also took measures to improve the collection of advance warnings of the arrival in Taiwan of members of terrorist organizations and information on the manufacture and trafficking of illegal biochemical agents and weapons of mass destruction. On the domestic front, an unknown group—or possibly an individual who a few days later committed suicide—attempted to assassinate President Chen Shui-bian and Vice President Lu Hsiu-lien in T'ai-nan on March 19, 2004, during their presidential reelection campaign.

Human Rights: Personal freedoms are guaranteed in Article 8 of the Republic of China constitution. The same article prohibits extralegal arrest and detention, requires that the organization making an arrest or detention shall make the charges known and turn over the detainee to an appropriate court not later then 24 hours after the arrest, and allows trials only as prescribed by law. Military courts are limited to the prosecution of persons in active-duty military service. In articles 10 through 16, the constitution guarantees a wide range of rights, such as freedom of speech, teaching, writing, and publication; freedom of privacy of correspondence; freedom of religious belief; freedom of assembly and of association; the rights to live, work, and own property; the right to present petitions, lodge complaints, and institute legal proceedings; and the rights of election, recall, initiative, and referendum. Article 23 stipulates that these constitutionally guaranteed rights shall not be abridged by law "except as may be necessary to prevent infringement upon the freedoms of others, to avert imminent danger, to main social order, or to promote public welfare." Taiwan's Code of Criminal Procedure provides that no violence, threat, inducement, fraud, or other improper means shall be used against accused persons.

According to the U.S. Department of State's human rights report for 2004, there were credible reports that police have occasionally physically abused persons in their custody and that such abuses most often occurred in local police stations where interrogations were not recorded and when attorneys often were not present. According to the government, instilling respect for human rights is part of basic police training, and the Central Police University, the Taiwan Police College, and police departments are strengthening human rights and legal education in the student curriculum and personnel training. Human rights groups have acknowledged these improvements. Prison conditions generally meet international standards, and human rights monitors are allowed in for inspections. However, conditions are crowded, and prisons are being expanded. An area that has been considered seriously problematic is violence against women, including domestic violence and rape. Taiwan is a significant transit point and, to a lesser extent, a destination for trafficked persons. Organized crime rings reportedly traffic in a small number of women for the purpose of prostitution. The majority of cases involve women from mainland China, Thailand, Cambodia, Vietnam and Indonesia.